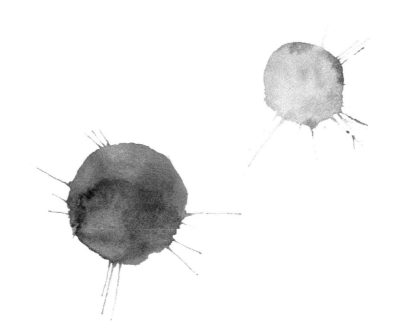

For my girls

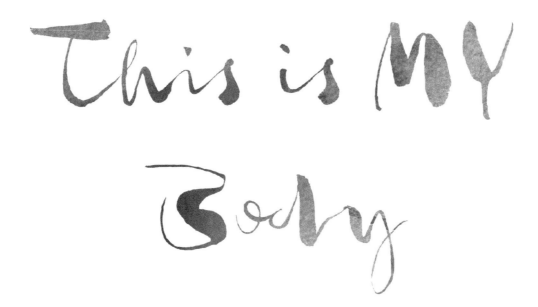

This is MY Body

Lil Carlé

Liuba Syrotiuk

This is MY body

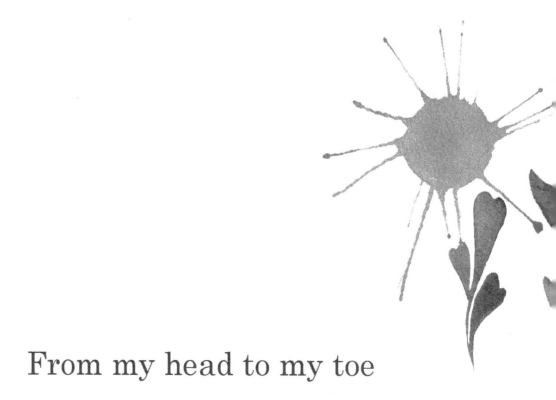

From my head to my toe

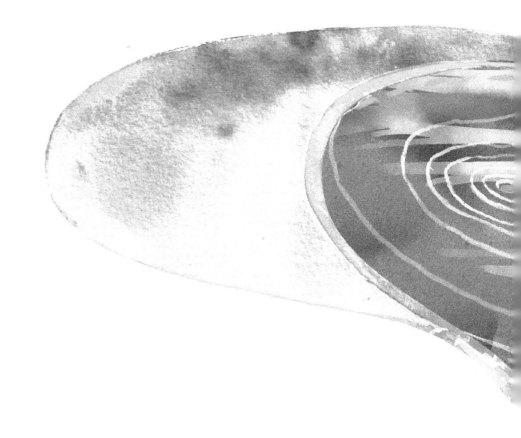

I'll choose what I do with it
As I move and grow

I'll choose what I wear

And what message is sent

And no one can touch me

Without my consent

This is MY body

In my bubble of space

I may let you share it

But at my own pace

I might not sit close to you
Or hold your hand
I might choose a high five
So please understand

This is MY body
I may give you the shoulder
Or choose other greetings
When I am a bit older

I'll choose who I cuddle
I'll choose who I kiss
But sometimes I'll want
To just give it a miss

This is MY body

I live in and own it
And no one will see it
Unless they are shown it

If I'm asked to do something
I'm allowed to say no
I don't have to have reasons
Because no is just NO

This is MY body
My body's my own
From the moment I'm born
Till the day I am grown!

CPSIA information can be obtained
at www.ICGtesting.com
Printed in the USA
BVHW021212220621
610213BV00006B/979